A MEDIEVAL FEAST

written and illustrated by ALIKI

HarperCollins*Publishers*

With respect, awe, and thanks to the medieval artists and
craftsmen whose illuminations, tapestries, and other works of art
are the basis for the illustrations in this book.

A Medieval Feast   Copyright © 1983 by Aliki Brandenberg   Printed in the U.S.A.   All rights reserved.

Library of Congress Cataloging in Publication Data   Aliki. A medieval feast.

Summary: Describes the preparation and celebration of a medieval feast held at an English manor house
entertaining royal guests.   1. Festivals–History–Juvenile literature.   2. Courts and courtiers–Juvenile literature.
3. Civilization, Medieval–Juvenile literature.   [1. Visits of state.   2. Courts and courtiers.
3. Civilization, Medieval]   I. Title.

GT3933.A54 1983   394.1′5   82-45923   ISBN 0-690-04245-0   ISBN 0-690-04246-9 (lib. bdg.)   ISBN 0-06-446050-9 (pbk.)

Published in hardcover by Thomas Y. Crowell

for Pat Allen

and for Mother, Helen, Vilma, and Peter –
remembering the annual feast....

t was announced from the palace that the King would soon make a long journey.

On the way to his destination, the King and his party
would spend a few nights at Camdenton Manor.
The lord of the manor knew what this meant.
The King traveled with his Queen, his knights, squires,
and other members of his court.
There could be a hundred mouths to feed!

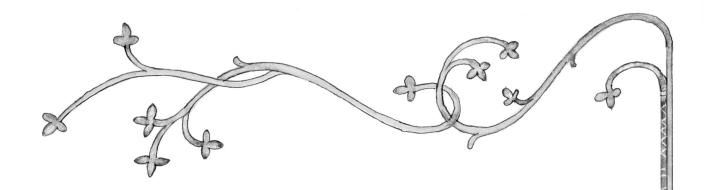

Preparations for the visit began at once.
The lord and lady of the manor had their serfs to help them.
The serfs lived in huts provided for them on the
    lord's estate, each with its own plot of land.
In return, they were bound to serve the lord.
They farmed his land, managed the manor house,
    and if there was a war, they had to go to battle
    with the lord and the King.

But now they prepared.

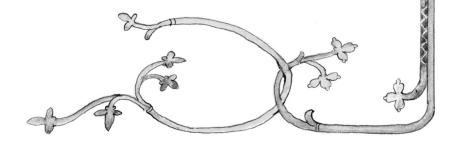

The manor had its own church, which was attended by everyone on the estate.

The Royal Suite was redecorated.

Silk was spun, new fabric was woven.
The Royal Crest was embroidered on linen and painted on the King's chair.

The manor house had to be cleaned, the rooms readied,
tents set up for the horsemen, fields fenced for the horses.
And above all, provisions had to be gathered for the great feast.

Hunting was a sport for the rich only. The wild animals that lived on the lord's estate belonged to him. Anyone caught poaching – hunting illegally – was severely punished.

BOAR

STAG

HARE

QUAIL

The lord and his party went hunting

Falcons and hawks were prized as pets.
They were trained to attack birds for their masters to capture.

CRANE

PHEASANT

PARTRIDGE

HERON

and hawking for fresh meat.

Serfs hid in bushes and caught birds in traps.
They set ferrets into burrows to chase out rabbits.

They trapped rabbits and birds of all kinds,
and fished for salmon and eels and trout.

There were fruits and vegetables growing in the garden,
herbs and flowers for sauces and salads,
and bees made honey for sweetening.

Trenchers were flat, coarse bread used in place of plates.
Peasants ate theirs, but the rich gave their trenchers to the poor.
Other breads were made of the finest flour.

Grains were ground into flour at the lord's mill,
and baked into trenchers and other breads.

Ale was brewed from barley, oats, and wheat.
Wines were made from grapes, often flavored with herbs and flowers.

Butter was churned, cheese was made,
    and ale and wines were ready in the brew house.
The King was almost there.

The kitchen was a separate stone structure built on to the main house.

The food was prepared in the great kitchen.
There were many cooks, and scullion boys to help them.

It was connected by a long passageway to the Great Hall, where the feast would take place. There were cupboards along the way to store the prepared food.

Pigs and deer and wild boar turned on spits.
Great pots of salted meat were boiled into stews,
    seasoned with spices only the rich lords could afford.

Swans and geese, heron and quail were roasted.
So was a rare beast called a Cockentrice.
It was really a capon and a suckling pig that were
    cut in half, stuffed, and sewn together again,
    each to the other's half.

A peacock was cooked, then reassembled with its feathers.
And four and twenty blackbirds were baked in a pie.

By the time the King and his party arrived,

everything was ready.

Tables and benches were set up along the sides of the hall.
A fire blazed in the center, and tapestries covered the damp stone walls.
The High Table stood on a raised platform. Near it was a display
of the lord's finest gold vessels.

The Panter brought in the King's breads, trenchers, and saltcellar.
The Ewerer tasted the water before he poured it over the King's hands.
Trumpets from the gallery sounded the start of the feast.

The guests swarmed into the Great Hall at half past ten
   in the morning.
Trumpets announced the King, who sat at the High Table
   with his hosts and other honored guests.
They washed their hands in scented water,
   and wiped them dry on a clean towel.
The Bishop chanted grace.
Then they ate and ate and ate.

There were no forks, but napkins were provided. They shared goblets of wine, and between courses the Ewerer appeared with water for them to wash their fingers.

They ate some of their food with spoons.
The rest they ate with their fingers.
They cut pieces from the meat the carver put on their
  trenchers with knives they had brought with them.

They used their little finger to sprinkle salt on their food.

Drums beat and trumpets sounded, as one surprise
    followed another.
They ate meat pies and fish tarts, and thick soups
    called Egerdouce and Bukkenade.
They ate boar's head and cow's tongue and
    Pudding de Swan Neck.

They ate a whole castle molded out of pastry, stuffed with
    meat, eggs, fruits, and nuts—and wondered how they managed.
Sweet and spicy sauces dripped into their trenchers
    as jesters, jugglers, and minstrels entertained them.
Course followed course, each ending with a fancy
    marzipan sculpture called a Subtletey.
After the guests admired them, they ate those, too.

They ate and ate until dark.
It was a feast fit for a king,
   and there would be more tomorrow.

The End

This Medieval Feast took place toward the end of the Middle Ages, about 1400. It is fictitious. But it could have happened in real life—somewhere in England, perhaps.

When the King announced he would visit, the lord was shaken. The expense of the preparations could cost him his fortune; it had happened to others. But he had no choice.

At least the lord could be glad it was summer, and there was fresh food. In winter, there would have been few vegetables and little fresh meat.

Farm animals were killed in late autumn, as there was not enough feed to last them through the winter. The meat was preserved in salt, or smoked, and eaten in stews during the cold months when people could not hunt. Though stews were served at this banquet, the fresh meat, fish, and fowl were far more welcome.

Medieval feasting was an art. Cooks not only prepared delicious food—they used their wild imaginations as well. They molded pastry into castles, sculptured desserts into kings and queens and elaborate scenes, all decorated with food paints. Live jugglers jumped out of puddings. Birds *were* baked in pies. But sometimes live blackbirds were hidden in the pie, to fly out at astonished guests. Each new dish was announced by trumpets and drums, and in between there was music and song.

The lord did his best. The King was given a feast to remember.

FOOD COLORS